I0188402

To:

From:

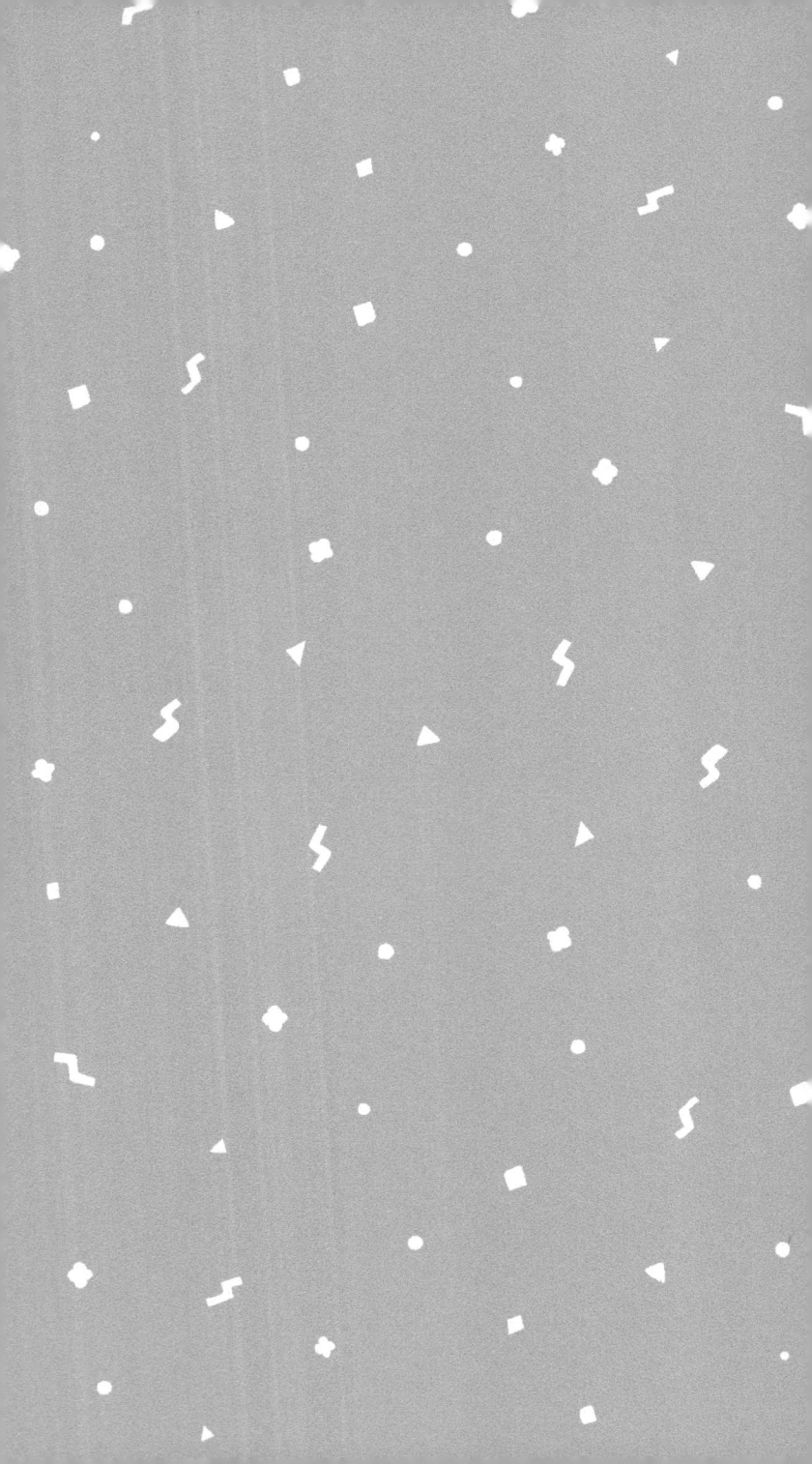

I Hope You

DANCE

Randa & Nadiath Adechoubou

Inspirational Quotes to Help You Enjoy
The Magic Of Life

IYA-OLOKA
PUBLISHING.CO

IYA-OLOKA

PUBLISHING.CO

First published 2020 by IJO,
an imprint of Iya-Oloka
www.iya-oloka.com

© Randa Adechoubou & Nadiath Adechoubou 2020

All rights reserved. Printed in the United States of America. No part of this book
may be reproduced, stored in a retrival system, or transmitted, in any form, or
by any means (electronic, mechanical, photocopying, recording or otherwise)
without written permission of the publisher.

Iya-Oloka does not have any control over, or any responsibility from any author
or third-party websites referred to in or on this book.

Library of Congress Control Number (LCCN) : 2020911478

Designed & Illustrated by Quynh Than & Thuy Com.
Printed and bound in the United States

ISBN 978-1-7352008-2-8
ISBN 978-1-7352008-1-1 (e-book)

Visit www.iya-oloka.com to read more about all our books , buy them and register
for newsletters and special offers. Copies are available at special rates for bulk
orders. For more details, contact bawo@iyaoloka.com

THIS BOOK IS FOR YOU.
KEEP ON DANCING.

To our parents Makarimi and Edwige Adechoubou. Thank you for teaching us how to dance in every season.

TABLE of CONTENTS

Hello!

Hello friend,

Thank you for picking up this book.

Regardless of how you got here, we are glad
to have you on this journey.

We designed this book so you can feel inspired,
motivated, and empowered to go after the life you
truly desire. No matter who or where you are -
mentally, physically, or spiritually - this collection
of quotes is for you. It's here to help you see
the power of your dreams.

To see the magic that is uniquely yours and help you
unlock it. As the great Maya Angelou once said:

"EVERY STORM
RUNS OUT OF RAIN."

So, if you are in a storm and are waiting for it to pass,
we hope this collection makes you dance through it.

Randa & Nadiath

01

LIFE IS BEAUTIFUL

I HAVE FOUND

THAT IF YOU

love life,

LIFE WILL

love you back

ARTHUR RUBINSTEIN

I don't
think of all
the misery but of
the beauty that
still remains.

ANNE FRANK

The best and most beautiful things in the world cannot be seen or even touched - they must be felt with the heart.

HELEN KELLER

OF THIS BE SURE:
YOU DO NOT FIND
THE HAPPY LIFE,
YOU MAKE IT.

THOMAS S. MONSON

THOSE
WHO DON'T
believe
IN MAGIC WILL
never
FIND IT.

ROALD DAHL

It's not
what we have
in life but
who we have
in our life
that matters.

J. M. LAURENCE

DON'T LET YESTERDAY TAKE UP TOO MUCH OF TODAY.

WILL ROGERS

Nothing

CAN DIM

THE LIGHT THAT

shines

FROM WITHIN.

MAYA ANGELOU

Life is from
the inside out.
When you shift
on the inside,
life shifts on
the outside.

KAMAL RAVIKANT

Life is a question and how we live it is our answer.

GARY KELLER

02

LOVE YOURSELF

The thing that is really hard, and really amazing, is giving up on being perfect and beginning the work of becoming yourself.

ANNA QUINDLEN

You are you.

Now, isn't that pleasant?

DR. SEUSS

WHERE'S
YOUR
WILL
TO BE
WEIRD?

JIM MORRISON

If you're always
trying to be normal
you will never know how
amazing you can be.

MAYA ANGELOU

If God had
wanted me
otherwise,
He would have
created me
otherwise.

JOHANN WOLFGANG VON GOETHE

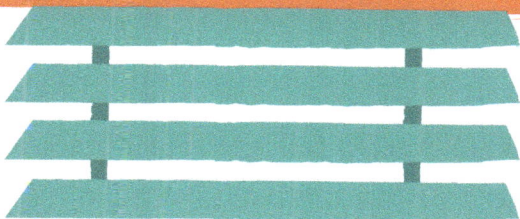

BY BEING YOURSELF,
YOU PUT SOMETHING
WONDERFUL IN THE
WORLD THAT WAS
NOT THERE BEFORE.

EDWIN ELLIOT

NO OTHER VERSION,
NO MATTER HOW
PERFECT IT IS,
WOULD EVER FEEL
BETTER THAN BEING
YOUR TRUE SELF.

EDMOND MBIAKA

We are so accustomed to disguise ourselves to others that in the end we become disguised to ourselves.

FRANÇOIS DE LA ROCHEFOUCAULD

YOU'VE BEEN CRITICIZING

YOURSELF FOR YEARS

AND IT HASN'T WORKED.

TRY APPROVING OF

YOURSELF AND SEE

WHAT HAPPENS.

LOUISE L. HAY

Be what you are.

This is the first step toward becoming better than you are.

JULIUS CHARLES HARE

03

BELIEVE IN YOURSELF

Close your eyes
and imagine
the best version
of you possible.

That's who
you really are.

Let go of any part
of you that doesn't
believe it.

C.ASSAAD

CONFIDENCE COMES NOT FROM ALWAYS BEING RIGHT, BUT FROM NOT FEARING TO BE WRONG.

PETER McINTYRE

I have never tried that before, so I think I should definitely be able to do that.

ASTRID LINDGREN

WE ASK OURSELVES,

*'Who am I
to be brilliant, gorgeous,
talented, fabulous?'*

ACTUALLY,

WHO ARE YOU NOT TO BE?

MARIANNE WILLIAMSON

If you are insecure,
guess what? The rest
of the world is, too.

Do not overestimate
the competition and
underestimate yourself.

You are better
than you think.

T. HARV EKER

We have to learn to be our own best friends because we fall too easily into the trap of being our own worst enemies.

RODERICK THORP

YOU CAN
HAVE ANYTHING
YOU WANT
IF YOU ARE
WILLING TO
GIVE UP THE BELIEF
THAT YOU
CAN'T HAVE IT.

DR. ROBERT ANTHONY

ALWAYS REMEMBER YOU ARE

braver

THAN YOU BELIEVE,

stronger

THAN YOU SEEM,

smarter

THAN YOU THINK.

A.A. MILNE

43

Don't limit yourself to the skies...

... when there is
a whole galaxy
out there.

BIANCA FRAZIER

04

YOU WILL SURVIVE

Brave are the ones
who fail and fall yet
they keep being kind.

Keep going strong.

Keep being at peace.

Keep spreading love.

ANJUM CHOUDHARY

NEVER LOSE HOPE. STORMS MAKE PEOPLE STRONGER AND NEVER LAST FOREVER.

ROY T. BENNETT

THOSE

THINGS

THAT HURT

INSTRUCT.

BENJAMIN FRANKLIN

50

Strength and courage aren't always measured in medals and victories. They are measured in the struggles they overcome. The strongest people aren't always the people who win, but the people who don't give up when they lose.

ASHLEY HODGESON

Be patient.
Sometimes you
have to go through
the worst to get
to the best.
Give time some time.

KAREN SALMANSOHN

IF YOU EXPECT LIFE TO
BE EASY, CHALLENGES
WILL SEEM DIFFICULT.
IF YOU ACCEPT THAT
CHALLENGES MAY OCCUR,
LIFE WILL BE EASIER.

ROB LIANO

When one door closes,
another opens; but we
often look so long and
so regretfully upon
the closed door that we
do not see the one which
has opened for us.

ALEXANDER GRAHAM BELL

CELEBRATE

ENDINGS

FOR THEY PRECEDE

NEW

BEGINNINGS.

JONATHAN LOCKWOOD HUIE

55

YOU ARE

SO MUCH

MORE THAN

WHAT YOU ARE

GOING THROUGH.

JOHN TEW

A SET BACK

IS A SET UP

FOR A

COME BACK

BISHOP T.D. JAKES

57

05

DREAM BIG

Start
where you are.

Use
what you have.

Do
what you can.

ARTHUR ASHE

NO MATTER WHERE

YOU'RE FROM,

YOUR DREAMS

ARE VALID.

LUPITA NYONG'O

There are some people who live in a dream world, and there are some who face reality; and then there are those who turn one into the other.

DOUGLAS H. EVERETT

Ever tried.
Ever failed.
No matter.
Try Again.
Fail again.
Fail better.

SAMUEL BECKETT

The only thing worse than starting something and failing is not starting something.

SETH GODIN

*There is only
one thing that makes
a dream impossible
to achieve: the fear
of failure.*

PAULO COELHO

The key to realizing
a dream is to focus
not on success but
significance - and then
even the small steps
and little victories
along your path
will take on
greater meaning.

OPRAH WINFREY

NEVER GIVE UP ON A DREAM JUST BECAUSE OF THE TIME IT WILL TAKE TO ACCOMPLISH IT. THE TIME WILL PASS ANYWAY.

EARL NIGHTINGALE

So many of our dreams
at first seem impossible,
then they seem
improbable, and then,
when we summon
the will, they soon
become inevitable.

CHRISTOPHER REEVE

IT'S NEVER TOO
LATE TO GIVE UP
WHAT YOU ARE
DOING AND START
DOING WHAT YOU
REALIZE YOU LOVE.

HANS ROSLING

06

CHOOSE
HAPPINESS

If you want
to be happy,
do not dwell
in the past,
do not worry
about the future,
focus on
living fully in
the present.

ROY T BENNETT

HAPPINESS

IS THE

secret

TO ALL BEAUTY.

THERE IS

no beauty

WITHOUT

HAPPINES

CHRISTIAN DIOR

HAPPINESS IS
A GIFT AND THE
TRICK IS NOT TO
EXPECT IT BUT
TO DELIGHT IN IT
WHEN IT COMES.

CHARLES DICKENS

DON'T WASTE A MINUTE NOT BEING HAPPY. IF ONE DOOR CLOSES, RUN TO THE NEXT WINDOW OR BREAK DOWN A DOOR.

BROOKE SHIELDS

Happiness is an inside job. Don't assign anyone else that much power over your life.

MANDY HALE

There is only one happiness in life. To love and be loved.

GEORGE SAND

Success is not the key to happiness. Happiness is the key to success. If you love what you are doing, you will be successful.

ALBERT SCHWEITZER

TO BE

content

MEANS THAT
YOU REALISE

you contain

what you seek.

ALAN COHEN

It isn't what you have, or who you are, or where you are, or what you are doing that makes you happy or unhappy...

... It is what you
think about it.

DALE CARNEGIE

07

FIND HOPE

I am

THANKFUL

*for all of
those who said*

NO

to me.

It's because of them I'm doing it myself.

ALBERT EINSTEIN

**Listen to
the musn't, child.
Listen to
the shouldn'ts,
the impossibles,
the won'ts.
Listen to
the never haves,
then listen close to me...
Anything can happen,
child. Anything can be.**

SHEL SILVERSTEIN

Hope can be
a powerful force.
Maybe there's no
actual magic in it, but
when you know what
you hope for most
and hold it like a light
within you, you can
make things happen,
almost like magic.

LAINI TAYLOR

I dwell in possibility.

EMILY DICKINSON

LET YOUR HOPES,

NOT YOUR HURTS,

SHAPE YOUR

FUTURE.

ROBERT S. SCHULLER

THE VERY LEAST YOU CAN DO IN YOUR LIFE IS FIGURE OUT WHAT YOU HOPE FOR. AND THE MOST YOU CAN DO IS LIVE INSIDE THAT HOPE. NOT ADMIRE IT FROM A DISTANCE BUT LIVE RIGHT IN IT, UNDER ITS ROOF.

BARBARA KINGSOLVER

No matter the number of times you fail you must be determined to succeed. You must not lose hope. Don't stop in your storm. Don't give up so easily.

TONY NARAMS

BUT DARLING...
IN THE END, YOU
HAVE TO BE YOUR
OWN HERO, BECAUSE
EVERYONE IS BUSY
TRYING TO SAVE
THEMSELVES.

C.T.

A lesson for all of us is
that for every loss, there is
victory, for every sadness,
there is joy, and when
you think you've lost
everything, there is hope.

GERALDINE SOLON

THE DIFFERENCE
BETWEEN HOPE
AND DESPAIR IS
A DIFFERENT WAY OF
TELLING STORIES FROM
THE SAME FACTS.

ALAIN DE BOTTON

08

EMBRACE CHANGE

THE GREATEST DISCOVERY OF ALL TIME IS THAT A PERSON CAN CHANGE HIS FUTURE BY MERELY CHANGING HIS ATTITUDE.

OPRAH WINFREY

The truth is, unless
you let go, unless
you forgive yourself,
unless you forgive
the situation, unless
you realize that the
situation is over, you
cannot move forward.

STEVE MARABOLI

CHANGE

THE WAY
YOU LOOK AT THINGS

&

THE THINGS
YOU LOOK AT

CHANGE

WAYNE W. DYER

Change is the law of life. And those who look only to the past or present are certain to miss the future.

JOHN F. KENNEDY

In any given moment we have two options: to step forward into growth or stepback into safety.

ABRAHAM MASLOW

You have this one life.

How do you want to spend it? Apologizing? Regretting? Questioning? Hating yourself? Dieting? Running after people who don't see you?

Be brave. Believe in yourself. Do what feels good. Take risks. You have this one life.

Make yourself proud.

BEARDSLEY JONES

Your life does not get better by chance, it gets better by change.

JIM ROHN

NOT EVERYTHING
THAT IS FACED CAN
BE CHANGED, BUT
NOTHING CAN BE
CHANGED UNTIL
IT IS FACED.

JAMES BALDWIN

You build on failure.
You use it as a stepping
stone. Close the door on
the past. You don't try to
forget the mistakes, but
you don't dwell on it. You
don't let it have any of
your energy, or any
of your time, or any
of your space.

JOHNNY CASH

THOSE WHO CANNOT

CHANGE
THEIR MINDS

—— CANNOT CHANGE ——

ANYTHING

GEORGE BERNARD SHAW

09

TRY AGAIN

THERE IS

NO FAILURE

EXCEPT IN

NO LONGER

TRYING.

ELBERT HUBBARD

FAILURE SHOULD BE
OUR TEACHER, NOT OUR
UNDERTAKER. FAILURE
IS DELAY, NOT DEFEAT.
IT IS A TEMPORARY
DETOUR, NOT A DEAD END.
FAILURE IS SOMETHING
WE CAN AVOID ONLY
BY SAYING NOTHING,
DOING NOTHING,
AND BEING NOTHING.

DENIS WAITLEY

I really don't think life is about the I-could-have-beens. Life is only about the I-tried-to-do. I don't mind the failure but I can't imagine that I'd forgive myself if I didn't try.

NIKKI GIOVANNI

JUST BECAUSE YOU FAIL
ONCE, DOESN'T MEAN
YOU'RE GONNA FAIL AT
EVERYTHING. KEEP TRYING,
HOLD ON, AND ALWAYS,
ALWAYS, ALWAYS BELIEVE IN
YOURSELF, BECAUSE IF YOU
DON'T, THEN WHO WILL?

MARILYN MONROE

IT MIGHT
HAVE BEEN DONE
before
BUT IT HASN'T
BEEN DONE BY
YOU

ELIZABETH GILBERT

Failure is just a resting place. It is an opportunity to begin again more intelligently.

HENRY FORD

Keep on going and chances are you will stumble on something, perhaps when you are least expecting it. I have never heard of anyone stumbling on something sitting down.

CHARLES F. KETTERING

No matter how many mistakes you make or how slow you progress, you're still way ahead of everyone who isn't trying.

TONY ROBBINS

IF I'VE LEARNED ONE
LESSON FROM ALL
THAT'S HAPPENED
TO ME, IT'S THAT...

... THERE'S NO SUCH THING
AS THE BIGGEST MISTAKE
OF YOUR EXISTENCE.

... THERE IS NO
SUCH THING AS
RUINING YOU LIFE.

... LIFE'S A PRETTY
RESILIENT THING,
IT TURNS OUT.

SOPHIE KINSELLA

117

10

SHOW GRATITUDE

Gratitude is the healthiest of all human emotions. The more you express gratitude for what you have, the more likely you will have even more to express gratitude for.

ZIG ZIGLAR

LEARN TO BE
THANKFUL FOR
WHAT YOU ALREADY
HAVE, WHILE YOU
PURSUE ALL THAT
YOU WANT.

JIM ROHN

Thank you is the best prayer that anyone could say. I say that one a lot. Thank you expresses extreme gratitude, humility, understanding.

ALICE WALKER

ACKNOWLEDGING THE GOOD THAT YOU ALREADY HAVE IN YOUR LIFE IS THE FOUNDATION FOR ALL ABUNDANCE.

ECKART TOLLE

Gratitude unlocks the fullness of life. It turns what we have into enough, and more. It turns denial into acceptance, chaos to order, confusion to clarity. It can turn a meal into a feast, a house into a home, a stranger into a friend.

MELODY BEATTIE

Enjoy the little things, for one day you may look back and realize they were the big things.

ROBERT BRAULT

IT'S A FUNNY THING
ABOUT LIFE, ONCE YOU
BEGIN TO TAKE NOTE OF
THE THINGS YOU ARE
GRATEFUL FOR, YOU BEGIN
TO LOSE SIGHT OF THE
THINGS THAT YOU LACK.

GERMANY KENT

DON'T PRAY

WHEN IT RAINS

IF YOU DON'T PRAY

WHEN THE SUN SHINES

LEROY SATCHEL PAIGE

No one who achieves success does so without acknowledging the help of others. The wise and confident acknowledge this help with gratitude.

ALFRED NORTH WHITEHEAD

Do not spoil
what you have
by desiring
what you have
not; remember
that what you
now have was
once among the
things you only
hoped for.

EPICURUS

See you later...

While we are at the end of our time together, this is not goodbye.

We hope you enjoyed the collection of quotes we put together for you. and we hope you continue to enjoy them as you embrace all that life has to offer. And most important of all, we hope they made you dance. To learn more about the "I Hope You Dance" movement, visit us at:

WWW.IYA-OLOKA.COM

THANK YOU

Thanks for reading!

We hope you found inspiration and positivity in this book, and hope that you will spread that good feeling to others around you. Our mission is to share joy and happiness in the world, and we know we can achieve that together.

We would also love to hear your thoughts on the book, please consider dropping a quick review at the retailer of your choice or reach us by email at:

BAWO@IYA-OLOKA.COM

Bye for now, and keep on dancing!

Randa & Nadiath

ABOUT THE AUTHORS

Nadiath Adechoubou is a wellness entrepreneur who wants nothing more than to help others. She loves meeting people, helping them discover what their unique gift is so they can nurture it, harness it, and share it with the world.

Hers is an explorer's heart. Having lived in several countries and met many different people, Nadiath has found that human beings all share the same base aspiration: the pursuit of happiness. That's why she has embarked on a journey to inspire and uplift herself and anyone she meets along the way.

Nadiath lives in Washington, D.C. She enjoys being active, cooking, reading, and spending time with her loved ones.

ABOUT THE AUTHORS

Randa Adechoubou loves to tell people what to do. Who doesn't ? A corporate strategist by day and a discerning foodie by night, she is passionate about helping people become the fullest expression of themselves.

A product of the 80s, Randa is a collector of experiences, a sun hater, life liver and a glow seeker.

When she is not spending time with her loved ones, you might find her trying new recipes, reading and dreaming of deserted and exotic far off lands. Randa's life's long motto? Shine and Thrive.

ABOUT THE PUBLISHER

IYA-OLOKA
PUBLISHING.CO

Iya-oloka is an independently owned publisher, specializing in books that tell relevant, uplifting, and powerful stories. We are on a mission to spread inspirational books that speak from the heart, and drive forward African lifestyle and culture.

At Iya-oloka, we are proud to produce and promote the highest-quality books that we hope will inspire generations of readers to bring about positive changes in their own lives and share that positivity with those around them.

Visit us at:

WWW.IYA-OLOKA.COM

www.ingramcontent.com/pod-product-compliance
Lightning Source LLC
Chambersburg PA
CBHW041822090426
42811CB00010B/1077

* 9 7 8 1 7 3 5 2 0 0 8 2 8 *